The Diary Young

poems

DASHIELL GREY

Copyright © 2023 by Dashiell Grey

All rights reserved. This book or any portion thereof may not be reproduced or used in any manner whatsoever, without the express written permission of the publisher except for the use of brief quotations in a book review.

Printed in the United States of America

First Printing, 2023

ISBN 978-0-9661200-9-7

Small Potatoes Press
www.smallpotatoespress.com

In Dashiell Grey's debut publication, *The Diary Young*, he attempts to weave modern and sentimental topics with an antiquated tone. This collection of poems follows no set track of topics; from religion, to philosophy, to love, to nature, to really anything—they are simply marvelings from a young mind.

There is no destination, for there is no journey. There is no answer, no question, no beginning or end to these poems. For no matter the topic, they persist beyond the page. They persist beyond resolution. And resolution is irrelevant to being.

The Diary Young is a glimpse into the personal diary of Grey -- and with that -- there is so much to see.

> "But I won't indulge until much later;
> The much later that is old age,
> And I will be prepared to state:
> I'd be willing to do it all over again."

> - "A Poem to a Subsequent Man"

TABLE OF CONTENTS

The Lanterns Assist the Darkened Path	10
Thou Shalt Love a Character	10
What Puzzle Permeates a Person!	11
Stranger! Stranger! Where Art Thou Now	12
Garments Bygone and Wish'd	13
A Delight Imbues a Fate	14
Fogged Flier	14
To What is Winter to a Wood Frog	15
The Long Parting	16
Marveling Hand	17
Admiration is a Volatile Alm	17
As Gradually as Sorrow	18
A Bull in the Month of May	19
'Twas a Vacant Lot-Thro' Ache-	20
Ofttimes is the Forest Green—	21
To Thee!	22
Many a Novel Sound in the Brush—Tonight	25
I Meander Walk Through a Door—For Guerdon	26
Where Stars Shine the Brightest	27
Love is a Jealousy Adorn'd	27
To Justify a Deed-Not Done	28
A Pard, Came Through the Pines	30
Art the Holy Secluded for Gold	31

Doth She Rise	32
Is Love the Honor Concluded	32
A Life Well Spent	33
A Dream—Like Many Others	33
Wary I Studied My Life, Abroad	34
A Breath Around the Mountain	35
Where the Stream Diverts	36
What Opus is This?	38
Threescore—I Have Been Away From Home	39
A Haunt Inhabits Nearly Every Bedside	40
I Reside in Hope	41
I Drift'd Far Far Out	41
A Burning Hour of Fusee	42
Ad Nauseam	43
When One's Not Pious-They Pretend	44
I Am Half	46
I Sank—Before Them All	47
I Died for Rapture—But Meager Was	48
I Survey the Passerby, Running	49
Bring Me the Sunset Upfront	50
Offhand—is the Lonesome Facet	51
Sheltered in Marmoreal Hall—	51
Life-Is the Note	52
In the Habit of the Darkness—	53
'Twas Qualms That Gave Us Away	54
Before Vision Was Used for Sight	55
My Jubilee	56
By the Waters I Decree	58
The Promised Land	59

I Chase Only a Star	60
What Is to Be of Their Ceiling?	62
Cadence Flows	63
Cain and Abel	64
Deer in Headlights	65
Thy Range and Regalia	66
Melody For the Brook and Stream	68
The Celebration of Rest	69
Wild Weeds	70
Irises Rising	70
The Fount of Revival	71
Let Alone a Nation	72
Habitual Despondency	74
Another Flower	76
I Left a Red Rose for Venus	77
Umbrella Magnolia	78
Hypocritical Burdeness	80
O Weary Walking Mile	81
The Accomplished Journeymen	82
Rubies and Diamonds	83
We Call That Spring	84
Exertion Once More	84
Love^9.	85
Swans	85
The Architect	86
Of Intermediate Life and Company	87
The Bridge	88
In a Field Behind Thy House	89
Venus	90

Simply Reminds Me	91
Watercourse	92
XIX	93
In Limerence	93
Evening Affairs	94
Mourning Doves Make Fools	96
Wild Wight	97
A Poem to a Subsequent Man	98
Diversion	99
Cardinals	100
A Not Seen Acumen	102
By Heaven	103
The Ostler and Steed	104
About the Author	107

The Life

THE LANTERNS ASSIST THE DARKENED PATH

The lanterns assist the darkened path
Until the path dost end
And then—light is eclipsed—
Fair blindness, without favor—
What doth I hath then?

And cease to recall
Herald annul the light
If thy eyes art shut—
What we shan't permit to shape us
Is remorse—benight—
E'en by conscious—
A gradual humbling flame
That came adjacent to our path
That was perilous—before name—

THOU SHALT LOVE A CHARACTER

This is my epistle to all and sundry—
That never corresponded—e'en to me—
The simple candor that nature ne'er hid—
To abide by others in care amid

My message is enacted
To me, and merely me to incur
But if thou respect eternity—
Thou shalt love a character—

WHAT PUZZLE PERMEATES A PERSON!

What puzzle permeates a person!
The solace resides away—
An intrepid from a troublesome door
Who—before haring—never knew its splay

Whose curb none haven't seen,
But just his portcullis—
Like looking through but never there
In some purloin paradise!

The passerbys appear more worrisome,
I occasionally speak to he
For assurance that it's merely the bars
And not the likes of me.

Feasibly comparable they are,
The honey and the bees—
Where they are impregnable
And shows no leisure guarantee

But my role is of deviance;
The ones that scan it most
Have never stepped a foot on his floors,
Not to query-friend the host.

The curiosity of those who wander about
Is led by positions gate—
For when they ask why I'm behind,
I answer—more curious is their state.

STRANGER! STRANGER! WHERE ART THOU NOW

Stranger! Stranger! Where art thou now?
Bereaved am I to be found—
A fabric yarn'd for kinship be—
I—ever since hadn't made a sound—

Thou discern a voice so distant—
Up through the immortal ring—
Where to rue would be of waste—
For absconded do I sing—

Who—essential merely to my soul—
Company wish'd would stay—
For who is more greatly concerned—
The onlooker or those who bear away?

GARMENTS BYGONE AND WISH'D

A novel companion for prosaic days
Is simple to descry
Than one of uniformity
For a maverick mind awry—

The garments a little too deceased—
To each his own display—
If the himation epoch is loosely felt
Than those of fleece—chambray.

Who is held liable—these spare times?
Ah! The aggravated pace!
The luminaries or the needless form—
So inadvertently take place!

A DELIGHT IMBUES A FATE

A delight imbues a fate
Blunderingly discern—
The Chevalier not remove his name—
Lest he beheld secern—

But peers and peerless endemic—
And eloquent—and inebriated—
Nay he drinks—to stay decorous bent
Or surely—he is lustrated!

FOGGED FLIER

My bird flies to thee—
The wind jostled trees—
"Wilt thou welcome me?"

My bird hovers hang fire—
O tree—look upon my fogged flier!

"I'll inhabit thee bough
And bide longest thy allow!

And judder me to collapse
From my nest onto the grass—

Say—trees!
Bear me!"

TO WHAT IS WINTER TO A WOOD FROG

To what is Winter to a wood frog—
This thought—merely a surmise—
Thought see—he overwinters then—
For exigency and not by desire
And dost thou think he revels so sweet—
Or that he laments his case—
Is the Winter his inspiriting vesture,
Or his forlorn embrace?

Within his cataphor is there reassurance
And is man's prudence so kindly resourced
That he honors whether he lives or dies—
And is man entitled to see it fit—
For he is buoyant year-round,
Or is he like that of a wood frog—
Teetering to rise—ne'er to make—
A sound?

THE LONG PARTING

'Twas conjecture they often spoke,
Between He, God and man—
Before the guide was greatly surmised,
Who earliest deduced then?

'Twas not I who presumably spoke,
Thoughts seldom turn to notion—
These acolytes expatiate themselves,
With the prevailing motion!

No conquest of time held accord,
Appareled it to be candor,
For many a flavor circumvent,
And palate present does mander.

'Twas the long parting e'er so simple.
Alas, headway has been thwarted since then—
But we hark back to this antique,
In lieu of forming again!

MARVELING HAND

As if I urged boorish bequest,
And bear upon my marveling hand—
A mediator converged unbounded,
Alas, I mold the essential who withstand-
And is this the inspiration they spoke—
The blue thwart'd by my foible—
And if I were to face attest'd flair,
Would I be advantageous and fall loyal?

ADMIRATION IS A VOLATILE ALM

Admiration is a volatile alm
Gifted from lack and cajolery
Upon palpable discern—by saints
Seemed as self antipathy
Where tramps dare not befall to
And frank lovers dare not see
A wavering house of worship
'Twas rumored to be.

AS GRADUALLY AS SORROW

As gradually as sorrow
The thrill dwindled elsewhere—
Too inconsistent to persist
The exchange was amiss there.

Some Serenity refined
And redefined itself—
As a stubborn quarreler—
Privy to themself—

The tiff drew itself in—
The after unknown was—
A gracious, yet inevitable grief—
That's own imploding—cause—

And thus, without proper reason,
Or a chance to prevail—
The exchange was a separation
To peace it once hailed.

A BULL IN THE MONTH OF MAY

A Bull, came through the alley,
I viewed him from afar—
His desafio readied he and I—
And he ran towards me to spar.

He hurled himself at me,
And faltered when banderillas struck—
And blood trickled down his broad neck,
Yet he still dashed toward me amok—

I turned my capote against him—
And he turned ever so fast,
And then came he careering,
Forward my back alas—

From the ground, I viewed his rapid eyes
That sprinted far and wide—
I was taken from the bullring
To mend my wounded hide.

I retire now at my hobby farm—
Where the box elders sway,
And the livestock I tend to
To keep me busy and gay—

And I cater to the cattle
Which I see nearly e're day—
And with the heifers and calves—
I tend to the Bull in the month of May.

'TWAS A VACANT LOT-THRO' ACHE-

'Twas a vacant lot—thro' ache—
That seldom—vesture of mind—
With many a circumstance—and risk—
That only stops—at curtain time—

'Twas the recruiters—she omitt'd
There—'twas to heed—permitt'd—
Then—self acquitt'd—
The vast roads became infinite—

Then lapsed—they became compact—
To her favor—orderly and set—
Then—prevalent—was her steps!
Ah! Look upon her kindred spirit—

The dog ear—ring—O'er again deliberate—
Her blue coat—hark—
And these maim'd boots make the mark—
Herself—nonplus—the arc!

The epoch ceased—now anew—
A man now—following—a few—
In reverberation and new brawl—
Too many oddments—to crawl—
For the road to be so small—
He walks the lot!

OFTTIMES IS THE FOREST GREEN –

Ofttimes is the forest green—
Ofttimes marigold or brown.
Ofttimes revises her own crest
When no life is around.
Ofttimes she nears her death
With thirty day links—
Outright—enough to recompense
With twelve links on the brink—
And man must fear his expiry—
For consistent are his ways!
And to border nature—from outside—
He emulates form today!

TO THEE!

"Lest I come and smite the Earth with a curse,"
"How doth the eager beaver be,"
"In the beginning when God created the heavens and the earth,"
I fumbled—did thou see?

Oh "increscunt animi!"
Oh Woolly disagree!
And oh "virescit volnere virtus"
Where I am muddling up thee!

Yawp to Emma Goldman!
Yawp to Voltairine De Cleyre!
Lauds, good fellow, for these heroines
Who stood virtuous foursquare!

Pilate, emulate Joseph;
Good Caiaphas, get on with palavers;
Say, Peter, reflective upon yourself?
Call the Apostles the engravers!

Don't take all of the blame, Adam,
It was Eve who tempted you,
So shalt thou taste my gala
And watch the liquor brew!

I viewed your trod so closely,
And followed behind sole in sole;
Such ineffable hope bequeathed
Upon me as if to gambol!

Unto my chamber
My commonwealth sets me leave;
As though my heart were stranded
From its former place on sleeve!

During my very own forum,
They made me believe
That I contain beneficial facets,
To encourage others to achieve!

In what matters were they talking;
Was I Inspiring or I ruth?
Was it all just nomenclature;
Or a baffling truth?

It was valorous Lief Erikson,
A voyage o'er from Iceland,
Who set where I shall live,
Not that Columbus fellow, a hasbeen!

If mortality is a frailty—
Then why do the divine
Die upon Olympus—
This notion has been resigned!

Our framers o'er hillside,
Supine on Cowpens win;
And tho' the remained cheer,
The winners shan't again,—

The band, O captain, shall play them,
In meager modus operandi,

And tho' we cannot hear them,
We appreciate what we can see!

'Tis the sook who is stubborn,
He fires until he has won;
But the perpetual paladin,
Fights not with cannon nor gun!

So long, E'erbody, so long;
Death calleth upon I;
Provide me all I need,
But let me stout-heartedly die!

In proof of our accord
Bear this "Voltairine De Cleyre,"
Lo, perhaps you shan't know her,
Perhaps I'm putting on air,

The souvenir of my being
Will great succor be;
Then, so long, Commonplace,
'Tis not so common without thee!

MANY A NOVEL SOUND IN THE BRUSH–TONIGHT

Many a novel sound in the brush—tonight—
A mere soul—they incite—
As an established walk—led astray—
Mystic—prefer to my excite—

A planet—too near to pursue—
Nor well-nigh—to reach—
Leaped from the secluded stars—
To meet in a plash on the street—

A high—high wind—shakes the tree tops—
And babels gust or leaves—
I attempt to separate the two—
But my attention is taken by thieves—

A returning home of several fireflies
To their abodes—light concealed—
My notice of these—shall I tell—
Would oft be deemed freewheeled—

Of foxes hosting soirees
With tea and stately waltzes—
Whose gowns and tuxedos bury their tails
'Neath the great balsas—

How am I to ne'er tell?
Alas—many omit to agree—
The world is full of wonderful sights
If you are willing to see.

I MEANDER WALK THROUGH A DOOR— FOR GUERDON

I meander walk through a door—for guerdon—
A door ne'er open nor enticing—
For which the body balks upon my person—
For a preference they are not sufficing.

Fallacious I may be not with reason—
For we may share alike good intention—
I meander through not in my mind—treason—
But that door to them seems to be dissension—

Perchance we are all seeking for selfsame—
But different doors allure us—
And lest those that fall short with much shame—
May impel them to shut the door—as a truss.

I feel for those who fasten the door—
And halt our voyage would be—
But room we have for you and more—
Come—meander walk through with me!

WHERE STARS SHINE THE BRIGHTEST

Achievement is held in the highest regard
By reluctant the heart—to achieve.
To apprehend such a discernible aim
Entails tenderest vive.

Not one of all the stars seen
Shine brighter than the rest—
Rather where one's stance shall be
Determines what is best—

As he who's quelled—beaten—
Has seen the brightest star—
Falls faster down the impassive sky—
Too heavy to hang afar.

LOVE IS A JEALOUSY ADORN'D

Love is a jealousy adorn'd—
With courtship to and fro
That dawdles to thy door
And then asketh thou to go—

Thole, thou perch on thy long haul'd perron—
At some strangers' null set!
Thou must maintain residence, green
And find another door to coquet!

TO JUSTIFY A DEED-NOT DONE

To justify a deed—not done
To draw from the water high—
Appear to him—the humbled land—
Yet such merit to turn awry—

And tho' in prosaic cadence—
A fable that Moshe would be
To suffice—a wrong set
To coincide with he—

Transcends indisputed tale—
Of Adam and Eve—or of Idit—
For punished—some figure or form—
By God's deft and eager wit

On Moshe—implement'd
With intriguing domineer
As frail wind—with leaves to shake—
To prove not as compeer.

Fault to retort—plainly Israelites'—
Provoked—Moshe—he was then—
But lest morale be thwart'd now—
'Tis not but himself to punish man

To conspire be he that is lowly—
'Twas to prosper amongst peers—
If one Moshe is condemn'd with such weight—
God —He will merely hear what one fears

But if many a fear—intimate to one—
'Tis what He struggles to grasp—
Shall be mark'd by no verdict—
And not fear of such wrath!

A PARD, CAME THROUGH THE PINES

A pard, came through the Pines—
Snow muted my view—
He leaped upon a marmot
And explored with his teeth, into,

And then, he rested an outcrop
In a stones throw alcove—
And then his kinsfolk came along
To nestle him commove—

He shared my prying eyes,
That descried the white abound—
They looked fierce and vigilant, I write,
That kept him safe and sound.

Like one that seeks a finer glance,
I advanced past the thicket,
But upon a twig that split, I stepped,
He hastened—from the sound like a cricket—

Akin to the snow that rose the earth—
A solitary commotion,
Or lantern flies, off the edge of stars,
Coincide, one without motion.

ART THE HOLY SECLUDED FOR GOLD

Art the holy secluded for gold
With her linen seldom told,
Facile as she!

Like her the company steal
Plaudits and dependent peal
For the day!

"Composed we are"—they convince!
For 'tis decompress amble away,
Not remain,

Forlorn is the saint however—
To merely ponder to recall
Grant profane!

DOTH SHE RISE

She riseth from the past—
Or she riseth from the present—
Her Revolution doth abating amends,
The dozes of the crescent—

The thoroughfare doth rest
And She blue heirlooms the earth—
Remains alas forlorn is She
To not see stars and merely people dearth.

Midstway to lain as the rising Night—
The Moon states that He keeper is—
Not people about mere stars far
And muted ennui that claims His—

IS LOVE THE HONOR CONCLUDED

Is love the honor concluded—
The precondition for what is then
And art fundamentals applied
To what is cheating when—
And since thou hath loved so dearly,
Why hath thy ribbon been repealed—
'Twas was it that thou pretermitt'd reason
To fall in love not heal'd.

A LIFE WELL SPENT

If I shall reach one hand 'fore slipping—
That would be a life well spent
If I shall shade one from some despot sun
Or help a vague one represent—

To find a broken bird
And remind it that it sings
Would be a grand event—
For—rest is easy when foretold
To me—That would be a life well spent.

A DREAM—LIKE MANY OTHERS

A dream—like many others—
Sojourns its merry way—
And amendable it is to find—
A haven for it to lay—

And abounded—is the dream—or shade—
And fruitless must be the squall—
That shall disperse the eager dream—
That is a guide to all—

I've flown such dreams throughout the sky—
Such winds—yet ne'er winced—
And—always—do I grasp the reel,
That I have been flying—since.

WARY I STUDIED MY LIFE, ABROAD

Wary I studied my life, abroad
Garnering—sifting evanesce
For what shall pique a stranger's interest
With O! belated pleasance.

I gave hindmost to the coterie
While prevailment—what was left.
I went one cool Autumn morn
And lo, my spare bereft—

'Twas not the boon companions—
'Twas not myself, a gaffe—
And from a blooming recollecter—
A languid mind, they chaff.

Regarding the thief—feasible—
Regarding I—more greatly considered—
Alas! Could be the numen, you know—
My line relies on the remembered!

Prohibit reflect o'er yonder—
Bounded is the brain—
Probable 'tis what is known
And mourning what can't remain!

Impairing that is to be true—
So I return to catch the grain—
Lackaday! I only have a sifter—
Arbitrarily, I collect what I can contain.

A BREATH AROUND THE MOUNTAIN

A breath around the mountain
Scouts ceaselessly through the year
Without e'er stopping—
A hamlet built here

Upon the breaths interweave
Through the highland Springs
Is where life omits
Apart from when stoles fling.

It gusts through the forges,
And about natures formation
To show all else that it resides
To privy those of ablation.

Then as scores lapsed,
Tranquil became the ben
And the villagers cheer'd
And disregarded the breath again—

But as forebears passed,
The glacier aloft grew
And collapsed upon all
And merely the breath knew.

WHERE THE STREAM DIVERTS

A spare man in the tall grass
At intervals speaks solemn—
You assuredly have seen him. Haven't you?
His regard prompt did—

The tall grass swaths the steady limb,
A narrow swale is seen,
Where he forges a flutter mill,
And goes again, water down the stream

But he questions what is a stream,
Without the waters exertion,
But he doesn't think more than that,
So he can ask a passing person—

He savors the streams clarity,
It tends to only north,
And wherever the brook diverts,
Is beyond what he has seen

DASHIELL GREY

Have I passed this stream thought I,
The end at where it disbands,
And have I seen this spare man—
The streams and man where they divert—

Several of native townsmen—
I know, and they the same—
I sorrow for them a dearth of sincerity,
But we indulge in promiscuity—

Our ways have been said repugnant,
And we speak that way of him,
As he tends to his fallow, solitary ways,
We portray him as the disarranged—

But never have I met this man ,
Up through where the streams meet
For he sees that the stream separates,
And to our oneness he's discrete.

WHAT OPUS IS THIS?

What opus is this?
What marvelous fanlight
Has become an overhead glance?
I photoed it—"florid"—in the wen
And fastened it—askance.

Virtuosos—'tis common practice—
Are commended concerning pundits.
But whether which the opus—
And whether which is merely mar
My perusal questions—I admit

THREESCORE–I HAVE BEEN AWAY FROM HOME

Threescore—I have been away from home—
Yonder—like a charnel on the rise—
I stared—through the broad glass—
And was removed there—edgewise

From the horseless carriage
That—once—had a stead—
And we lumbered the stone walk—
Upon the deck—brought my knees.

I loused up at my mettle—
I recalled perching on the stoop
To evade maelstrom—lingering inside—
And to not take place—cooped—

I clutched the peristyle—firm—
And spurned my departing back—
While the others attempted to induce
Me—like stream from stickleback—

The dweller piloted—upon the towpath—
And hollered upon my weary sight—
Lo, she prevailed standing in scare
As I headed towards her door—all might—

I contoured to the lock—my hands—
With hastened hesitation—
And opened it—taken aback—
Assured—by lack of restoration—

A HAUNT INHABITS NEARLY EVERY BEDSIDE

A haunt inhabits nearly every bedside—
Yet she undisturbed—
For his occupation—this—
Peculiarity not occurred—

Queer would be, a passing word
From an inert ghost—
What shall bestowed upon his host
That is of any note—

Queer would be, to mean a word,
Deemed a scornful embrace—
That a host could scold from her lot—
In a disenchanted place—

To recollect a ghost, his flesh there—
Alas, 'tis not the same—
For bare is he—aware is he—
That bygone—he was not released—

O Woe!—our host has newly passed—a soul—
Indwells with our ghost—
At last—parley they sorely enact—
To enjoy their shared post—

I RESIDE IN HOPE

I reside in hope—
For such a broad abode—
One can't only one—
For one mustn't have stowed—

Of halls as the megarons—
Qualms cannot reach—
And guides prevalent
They—the tenets who teach—

Of foundations—they tend—
My role—hark and versed—
The benefaction my eager hand
To collect and intersperse—

I DRIFT'D FAR FAR OUT

I drift'd far far out—
Outwith me beyond the sea,
Pass'd the wakeful rise and fall
The rhythm that continues when I call—
Oh! Stop thy duty if thou please!

The swell I learn'd to ride—
Prevail'd poise as I had no choice
But to tumble down into its throng—
In which motionless I heard its sub rosa song—
"Oh! Stop thy movement, sink deep from my voice!"

A BURNING HOUR OF FUSEE

Hazy is the redress—'tis meager compared now,
The fog latest—'tis easier to find—
Overwhelms the rabble from what is endemic—
For sentiments rule merely what burdens are to bind.

The proceeding is not trivialized—
Alas—I can't discern the sight
And what differs a howl and zephyr
From mending my ruptured plight.

O, who is to worry? Who is to blame?
Ah! the proletariat that once offered lee,
Now dismisses my forever burning soul
For a burning hour of fusee!

AD NAUSEAM

If I shall have it when I'm dead—
I will withstand through;
If at the moment a limp finger hangs—
It shall be in the hands of due.

Musn't count the inadequate times—
'Tis joy I cannot consider;
For though those times pass muster mo—
'Tis overall I do configure.

Think of it, the coterie and me—
Ad nauseam 'tis to see;
After through a door which I shall face,
Another door is open, due to be.

WHEN ONE'S NOT PIOUS-THEY PRETEND

When one's not pious—they pretend
To be the abreast—I know,
Or seek to be the one who seeks—
Alas—not privy ample for show—

With castle in air see through—
Holding tight
Their want—void of king—
Vacant might—

Discarded of the autocrat—
Burdensome—or onerous—
A convention sorely pleases—
Omitted be the ponderous—

I could not try—to do—
For there is no date
That firms what was contrived
When what's due is late—

And you—could you hope too
To see me—rise—
And comparable be—
Wavering advice—

Nor could I know—for you—
Because your eye
Would deter with mine—
Closer your horizon line

Is to mine—and foreign
Upon my bygone skies—
Find a medium of happiness—
To part would be bittersweet to I—

They'd determine me—how—
For you—first and true—I know,
I seek to—
You do not—

Because you bewitch'd might—
And I had no more rigor
For tawdry zest
As slicker

And would you be high, I'd be low—
Though my haze—
If so thin—
I shall wait—

And were you—high—
And I—shallow to be
Where you certainly are not
Locus'd—brought down for me—

'Tis bittersweet reunion—
Shall we part once again
With two thrones engaged
That horizons are—and orison—
Mine—merely for your sake
Which keeps me pious bespake—

I AM HALF

I am half wrong half right about what I entail
Or whatever it is that I needed;
For there's new debauchery of the common touch,
To which was sorely heeded!

Inebriated of introspection—I am I say—
Slurring speech as I am waking—
Riveted—thro' reminiscent of gaffe
Yet the astute is clear after I'm forsaken

When the cards are all played on the table
And my hand is empty yore—
Is when the prospect of quiescent brings forth
Or the option to pick up more!

Till Fragonard expels some secret state
And swing—my wayward dove
I shall be unassuming and woefully prim,
Before the secret state of love!

I SANK–BEFORE THEM ALL

I sank—before them all—
Therefore they sank with me—
I discern'd with ascription bias—
That they shall rise—to plead.

I heard no required return—
That would have risen me—
Yet my film dissolved—with scrutiny—

And when they understood—
I felt loved yet again—
I met them—
Beseeched to beseeched —

They told me finest—all rivers must flow
Thro' a greater body—
No freshet so strong
To not flood over so—

I told them reciprocal rapport
Where reachings grew—
In which weight was withdrawn
And then grounds pursued—

And so with the bijoux'd scrutiny—
Progress'd the torrent slow—
And in ways I did not know—formerly—
I let their rivers flow—

I DIED FOR RAPTURE–BUT MEAGER WAS

I died for rapture—but meager was
My assumption of paradise
When one who passed off indulgence
Adjacent to my lapse—gratified—

He disclosed warmly "acquainted with demise"
"I ask you to come again" I replied—
"You died ample—was it burdensome?"
""Twas obverse—insatiable"—I descried—

And so, he laughed, I felt a fool—
And admitted that I was laughing too—
'Till conversation was enfeebled by weeds
And towed me down—deeper—for someone must succeed—

I SURVEY THE PASSERBY, RUNNING

I survey the passerby, running—
And roaring through near arbor—
And I know prior to her unveiling
Through trees—her sound is before her

In abiding intervals—she laps beeline—
And halts merely for my esprit—
But as I garner constituents—she
Collects others—she can't determine me—

And then, the collected beckon me
To entrain with their drinking song—
I voice I'm imminent—sorely desired—
But my muster—gathered too long—

And she elapsed before my array—
Too eager to hang fire—
I do tho' near e're day
But circadian leads me to enquire—

BRING ME THE SUNSET UPFRONT

Bring me the sunset upfront,
Reminded I'll be it rises
And say 'tis akin hue,
Show me how lasting the sun projects—
Show me how tenebrous the night is—
The curtain of the moon—I'll reveal to you!

Send me a finch bundled
In mediums of vibrance
That flies among modish forthwith—
And alongside me an honest sparrow sits—
Which I have bestowed upon you—not subsidence ,
And we shall be reminded—twain herewith!

Also, who piloted me to sea,
Also, who conducted the pliant squall
That encroached on us with supple moves?
By Mo of wavering tranquility—
I favor the accord to all
And composed am I for the rooves!

And who built this bungalow for me
And latched the doors so tight I shan't beat
My soul cannot walk?
But speak not of alas, various mentioned I do see—
And the limbo of sun and moon shall meet—
And these possibilities I shan't balk!

OFFHAND–IS THE LONESOME FACET

Offhand—is the lonesome facet
Used by the sorrowful and sore—
Whose testament—a futile hand—
That denies the residing 'fore—

To tell it is a dynasty—broad and aware—
Yet the walls are deemed stiff—
What comfort 'tis for the few with key—
To walk through the gate—without tiff!

SHELTERED IN MARMOREAL HALL–

Betwixt conquering and comfort—
Sheltered in marmoreal hall—
Unblemished by the aging sun—
Unadorned by a pall—
Rest the gentle habitants of slumber—
Docile to their fall.

Glorious the years,
Unaccompanied by those asleep—
Palaces sculpt themselves to rise—
And others trounce steep—
And azure—the coursing row—
Some carefully stowed deep—
And some discarded off—
As silent as nights creep!

LIFE-IS THE NOTE

Life—is the note
Rather than erudition—
For all that is vital
Is merely creation—

Possibly—we go—to search
From our mansard stay—
But sterling—unto sterling concurrent—
Than endorse—to mislay—

Thought belongs to yesterday—the giver—
Which shall prevail through end—
But essence dwindles as corporeal plan—
'Tis inadequate to mend—

'Tis the obligation of the thorn
To tend to the roses welfare—
But taper the kind of reverence
Would not be the two to share.

IN THE HABIT OF THE DARKNESS—

In the habit of the darkness—
The gleam is stowed away—
Not because we have lost such light
But because we shelter the day—

At intervals—We speculative step
Into the mere hue known—
Then—adapt our eyes to the dark or
Light the way—we're prone—

And 'tis true of unique—darkness—
Whether 'tis dusk or eventide
Of the mind—no phare about
Or star—as a guide—

The bold and valorous—clumsy—
They miss a step—walking home—
Those dependent on their concealment—
Miscreants in their catacombs—

Darkness—either is a virtue—
Or we are afraid of what we might find
When we uncover the daylight—
It may seem easier to be purblind.

'TWAS QUALMS THAT GAVE US AWAY

'Twas qualms that gave us away
Amongst the reeling wit
In a fugitive fury of pique,
Until its dust could sit.

A chimera left lapsed,
Is a shadow gone,
That makes clovers ensue,
While it feels as weight had spawn.

BEFORE VISION WAS USED FOR SIGHT

Before vision was used for sight—
I liked so to see
Along with all fellow, that can—
I lament the after glee—

But shall it be told to me, Now,
That I may have Uninvolved Sight—
I apprise thee that my Heart
Would shatter, for I'd prospect of might—

The convivial kiss—know no more—
The intention not learn'd—
Before my eyes—
As much unlettered, as I could enjoy—
A life blind would be more wise—

To view the Sun without jeopardy—
A Pard, not look in line—
For mine—to see all things, in every way
Would be a privilege to incline—

So fruitful—the world—would be
With merely sight of soul—Then
If I were bestowed another chance
I'd say is there an again?

MY JUBILEE

Me! A catalyst! my pliable specs
In such an impulse for a wreck!

Me! Notion! leaden motion
That anticipation to raise demotion!

The nonpareils shan't forget
'Tis hitherto imperatively set.

My jubilee intent to stay
'Tis that I am remembered that very day—

My largesse to all, O yes, shall it be
That my name shall transcend me.

The Death

BY THE WATERS I DECREE

Along the Schuylkill river and the Delaware
The eager men were dancing, singing farewell
With the helm lying dormant
The forecastle cramped
Forty thousand spread among the ships
Empty are the ramps

But nobody lamented
Everybody drank
The Crystal streak waters
Or the cities metropolis flanks

Along Paper Mill Run and Acheron
The eager men handled raw industry
The Romans vended the fauns of the creek
Racing their chariots
And the river adjacent is to life, less than lustrum
but more than the spree
Washed themselves in embroidered waters
Running from something
Running from decree

But nobody lamented
Everybody drank
The Crystal streak waters
Or the cities metropolis flanks

THE PROMISED LAND

The burning desire for the promised land
To March through the restless scorching sand
The early sun and the late moon
One desired when the other is aboon
In a cycle that matches a misanthropes whine
Patents the day's conquest of time
To hinder the coverage we make on foot
The promised land is there

I CHASE ONLY A STAR

O star - the brightest one e'er seen,
We vouchsafe your elevation outright
To some anonymity of the mountains,
It will prevail to say it's gone,
Since your mein is apparent as your soul,
But I trust you'll return to the East End.
Some memory becomes blemished with desire.
But to be stark reticent
According to your cache is unjust.
Divulge unto us so we can pursue
By bond and often study when the morning arrives,
But now we must learn.
I speak! and you? You ask "what for?"
But divulge! And you say "I am ablaze."
But speak with lowdown and facet.
Don't say 'I am ablaze,' say 'I consist of…'
Embrace us so we can fathom.

Verse us with your atoms and your gas.
Yet, we are let down by what we learn,
But do speak while there in the sky.
And stalwart as the Meteor Crater.
Light - not even faint from behind the mountain,
It does not matter for our word or fact.
"I chase only a star, but alas this one is reluctant."
I turn my back to the light, and I see before me,
Upon the ground, the shadow of a star.
So when infrequently you catch a star,
You must realize it shines aloof very far,
And it's vast indifference to realize severance,
We are not to blame and must stay decorous.

WHAT IS TO BE OF THEIR CEILING?

The gods are drinking again;
A rough night
Of playing a round of
Egyptian Rat Tail
Spilling their voices through
The hollow walls of Heaven
I can hear them through the
Floor & ceiling
Their floor is my ceiling
Their walls are my walls
And occasionally, the gods
Will get in a quarrel
Spilling their booze and
Knocking their Cubans on the floor
Setting the sky on fire,
Sometimes it leaks through
And we get a taste
And to not what we expected,
It does not taste so sweet.

CADENCE FLOWS

The land was ours and then ours and then theirs.
She; the natural headway; let us settle upon her earth
    before we were of earth herself.
What was sought after was seeking itself, thus we land
    where we land,
Amongst the colonies and after, departing from ourselves,
And yet saying 'them' and 'their',
And what we were was 'us' and 'we' and 'our'.
Somewhere, further along, we sanctioned yet again,
Withholding peace because we didn't know peace was an
    option
And it still isn't, but we have embellished what peace
    means.
In partial was reluctant to repeat yet again,
For workers from the East went West, and were called
    'them' and 'their',
And found conservation a sin from the honest,
Now, years further, conservation has been misconstructed,
And is the enemy of the people. Both parties; their parties.
    And here I go,
Claiming to be ethically affluent, yet I refer to 'they' and
    'them'. O How the cadence flows.

CAIN AND ABEL

East of the border, to some it wouldn't matter
To harvest in the clatter
I thought I was Moses but I was really Cain and Abel
It wasn't a divine number
I was the number
And I thought I wouldn't be able
To reach out to the name
That I wouldn't be able to holler
But surely, I thought, it was merely a name
But still, I couldn't swallow
With the impending sound of willows
But there was no silver lining
Only foreseen objectionable dining
But alas, it wasn't you, I was Cain and Abel

DEER IN HEADLIGHTS

From which road is this my travels flow
Curling around the finger of God, I know
My destination will have to wait
For I see a deer in headlights mounted in snow.

My rationale ponders for none are astir
To become mirrored like the deer
Between the cedars and the stones
We both show no signs of fear.

The smoke reminds me to move along
As if my path is expectedly very long
The only other reminder to me
Is the silent night of the wary fawn.

The deer is divine, sudden and set
But off he goes able to forget
And off I go unable to regret
And off I go unable to forget.

THY RANGE AND REGALIA

Recitative thy seams exterior
Thee ferry through the rough inclement Winters, the day
    rising from the horizon
Thy range and regalia, thy steam arising from the stack,
    coating the foregoing sky with ample color
Thy carts expanding from one side of the line of sight to
    the other
The body, a glistening paragon of black paint, steel, and
    ornate pattern
The measure and metrical odyssey that is natural sound
Thy obtruding through the open snow-ridden landscape
Thy passengers carelessly organizing their manner in thy
    formal enclosure;
Not representative of the locomotive; a juxtaposition of
    most people even
The pilot protruding out, clearing away nothing but
    halcyon air
The valves, the gears, the wheels only moving forward;
The cars following behind, like sheep to a shepherd,
The modern contraption, succumbing to modern times;
Merely a moniker thou hath to satisfy;
For once fancy the modelesque stimulus and coalesce
    balladry,
Even as I withstand thee

With tempest and battering air; corresponding with the vast
    bleakness of the open country,
By day; from sights, a sheer acknowledgment of a
    contrasting specimen;
Races the train entity along the open country;
A black stallion; picking up snow with its legs, equal of that
    to the train

The passengers of the cars; looking at the stallion in awe,
Harmonize their excitement with gasps; thou unnoticing,
    speeding along
The horse snorts and looks straight ahead, much like the
    locomotive;
Yet not carrying along a herd, less liability, and more
    authority;
Owning the vast landscape for it has no tracks that guide
Manufacturing thyself unable, but able to be greater, in thy
    own time
The locomotive lets out a lawless, mad cry into the open air,
(Urbane and reverent noise, yet; shocking to the untamed,)
And the stallion, out of fright, turns left instead and
    continues elsewhere,
Through the vast open country and through the harshness
    of Winter,
The locomotive has trivialized yet another relic wishing to
    remain

MELODY FOR THE BROOK AND STREAM

Upon the mast of the river head
She wanders through the waters
And she shifts through like some thread
I caught a glimpse of her one morn
While bathing in the silver streaked waters
I heard her song while she did the same
Bathing under the sunlight's quarters
I made myself known and with shock
She saw me sitting on a mossy rock
While the streams pushed past my ponderous inferences
It was in our own nakedness and bewilderment we found our differences
I could not sing for I knew no song
And I knew she wouldn't stay for long
So I asked her an infatuated query:
"Be my singer; bring thy song"

THE CELEBRATION OF REST

This is the rain we've been waiting
for, O comrades,
thy unimpeded rest unto the quiet;
Noveling the books, the arts, the
work prior, the teachings of all levels
done,
Now left in their individual rooms to
 conquer;
And thee reposing onwards, at the
 fore, conquering thy rest, as the rain
gives a pardon,
And deriving the feat thou
cerebrate;
The celebration of rest

WILD WEEDS

Savor the pace of transcendental nature
To where a wild weed may grow beyond expectations;
If given the time to do so,
For transcendental nature cannot be rushed or pushed
    beyond its capacity at that time; but it will, eventually
And love all things natural for they have no aim of morality
And if you grow with transcendental nature too perchance,
You may find your calling;
which of course will be especial and solitary
but don't let the solitude delineate what you stand for in
    order to grow
Because remember,
You have no aim

IRISES RISING

"Oh, stand tall" says the white lily
"Some weep before me and some stand tall
You rise from the earth and die in the Fall
Your bulbs shan't be planted in a gardeners home
You are so wild, so natural and combed
Your blue Corollas jut out, oh how it mangles
With capturing light between your petals
The stems swearing to drag your beauty down
Into your home, into your ground"
"You needn't say such things" cried a blue Iris
"We know of our fate, we know that we're pious"

THE FOUNT OF REVIVAL

Château de Chenonceau during the Great War
Is the most majestic castle
She tended hearts and bleeding soldiers
Amongst the waters, the orchids, and the women
For she is the Castle of the Ladies
The springtime waters fly above the lilies
Besides a violin-
Lays a turreted pavilion
Besides a cello-
Lays a tower
Besides a harp
Lays a monumental entrance
Halls with great Flemish tapestries
Marble corinthian pillars; a beautiful foundation
Wood that appears as gold
Portraits of nobility
She is the port of connection
One— more world centered
One— primarily devoted to religion
She lies between eras
She lies between grace

LET ALONE A NATION

A great Nation making it public,
I can only say to myself that I; with a mind that is merely a bulb,
Can see the fault in the Nation's steps, which states there is no appreciation;
As if I am benefiting, let alone the Nation
And I refuse nothing, and welcome all, inside my Nation where I can emulate structure.

These grounds, which have become familiar, but not ample enough;
For me to wander more domestically, yet there, I have not come accustomed to yet,
And the quarrel with the great Nation is that the great Nation surpasses many a score
And I; just short of two.
What the Nation is, is what the Nation does, for it announces:

We are striving to prosper and to prosper is to strive
We are relentless and persistent in our efforts, to where movement is of no bay
We are managerial within ourselves and disclose nothing of the concern; for the truth shall diminish one's name, less or more, will they respect a truthful Nation?
We are the only Nation that perceives ourselves, and none other can reprimand; nor can I,
For words of a distressed sister Nation can't privy my lovely structure.

Whatever is told, whatever isn't, evades the Nation's desire to continue forward.

Have thee thought of other ways a great Nation can progress; infinite and supreme;
Beneficial to all, and to thyself?

HABITUAL DESPONDENCY

A voice so frail called out recurrent counsel:
'The poets, the artists, must let us imagine peace,
to depose what is prevailing,
habitual despondency is not productive,
the people needn't be reminded of their needs which is the
    stimulus of notion, and notion is an ineffective action to
    which repetition occurs."
Then another voice cried out amongst the crowd:
'But peace mustn't be disposed of,
rather the likeness of poets and the artists,
for we need to be reminded of what prevails for ourselves to
    prevail ahead,
peace does not merely exist on paper.
And the notion to cease motion is to pacify need!
Idealistic escapism is a siren song!"

"But peace is like a song, it can be sung in a myriad of
    ways,
What you say may be to your liking, but not to mine,
For I've heard of trial and error, and the people are tired,
    and most have been thriving without consideration for
    what may be best,
they are currently living are they not,
to me and the goodwill of the people."

"The poets and artist make us desire, and desire is kin
to inaction for most would call themselves crazy, adjacent
    to something they don't want to fight for, for there is a
    collective agreement, yet not collective action, you don't
    lead with promise, you lead with action!"

"The prosody of peace is implied with hope", called out
    another voice from amongst the crowd,
"action is not relinquished when promised, nor is desire, it
    is the will of the people that must arise from calamity,
    impulse adjacent, when there is no movement, there is
    no living thing,
which forms with or without tragedy,
and as a will, it shakes to and fro - but are you willing to
    surrender your time for the sake of peace?"
And as that was said, people trampled on each other and
    the place uproared with protest.

ANOTHER FLOWER

Another flower has been plucked,
In the warm embrace of spring,
A precarious embrace, but with upright intention,
To shield from the florist;
But Spring can't promise a thing.

But the pervasive pangs of the winter chill,
Casts as a reminder unto my window sill,
When in Spring hath thou e'en seen such a sight,
When those once blooming are dying.

And in the wake we mourn adrift;
For those that mourn are frightened stiff;
And have not encountered that type of rift,
Between those that are dead and dying.

And no matter how hath thou,
Ye all feel the shared mumbling fears,
That are briefly mentioned amongst thy peers,
And then disappear when no one's trying.

Yes, another flower has been plucked,
From it's uncertain shroud of dirt;
And now can no longer be scared of hurt,
For thou art dead and others - hurting.

I LEFT A RED ROSE FOR VENUS

I left a red rose for Venus—
And went against the tide—
'Twas while she was sound—asleep—
Success—and the differences I tried—

I—Mars—was championed then—
Not by right—but by wisdom—
And e'er since the fall—twice now—
Adoration and reverence—withheld from—

'Tis where the narrative varies—
Was all that could be done—
More tragic than that of mythology—
In word—more honest—finespun—

UMBRELLA MAGNOLIA

At the riverfront,
    Its dark, silken silver strokes
        the shaded verdant earth,
            Its leaves,
to and fro with the wind,
    Cover the multitude
        Of scenes beyond
            The Magnolia tree -
  It's trunk
      Belabored and hidden,
         is the prerequisite casket
For the tree's dying life.
In honest Philadelphia,
    In frank Philadelphia
        She is left unbothered
           In her own self,
                And is content to be,
And from her death
    She will stand the test of time
        As a passing glance at life
            to rest, and prosper apologue,
That if one is truly honest,
    Their image will be preserved,
        And not embellished, nor ornated,
            And will simply be,

And to discover the Magnolia one day,
    Maybe a child will claim it's theirs,
        And it's leaves sinking from heaven,
            Will bring some world to him.
The leaves sink once more,
    To drink the previous days rainfall,
        That the grass has collected,
            And mutual care upon the living and dying.
But then I remember:
    Death in fact, comes before life,
        to others that is,
            for others that is.

HYPOCRITICAL BURDENESS

For sixteen years
I've held a grudge against paper and
the bareness of inspiration that is void of all
      Ingenuity and
Emptiness for many an abstraction occurs
And never writes me back
When I cast my line
      Into its undetermined
Pages of blank canvas
Which is less than intriguing but astoundingly
Useful to diminish abstraction
      And prosperous to reverberation
But nothing occurs when I try
And the pages are just pages to think of an intention
Much like inspiration and how it's merely a notion of ideas
      Sixteen years
And again this evening per usual
I am fronted by the likes of my ideal that
Has a loose promise for my
      naive mind
Which forms the facets of my
Intuition that is smarting and abrupt whenever
A blank page offers itself to me in
      Marked fragments
From hour to hour I think
Of only when I will begin.

O WEARY WALKING MILE

First, O weary mile; do thou wander without me,
Through the acreage and down the weary stream,
Crossing the river mile, and uprooting the walking mile?
Do thou make my trip more arduous or less - shall I cross both to see;
Or save time and choose one? Yet,
Which mile is prudent the most? O dear me shall I walk both?
Yes, I think so. I shall trek both stream and road.
And upon those, contrasts shall content -
Yes, but what of the stream and road? What of them?
Will they respect the likeness of my curiosity?
Should they?
Will I sojourn or will I continue?
It is now that I have made up my mind;
I shall cross the river mile, and then continue the walking mile, for a new destination is afoot

THE ACCOMPLISHED JOURNEYMEN

Here I am - hand and foot;
Noiseless in the vast complexion of the ness.
Exposed are the paths and trails, as if I have been here
    before.
Directionless for;
One too many times I've come across this ness when the
    paths' were merely brush;
And thus, a way to clear them-
Ever growing high once, now cleared before I

And you O journeyman whomever you shall be;
You paved a path, for me, your intention, yet your
    execution is fruitless compared to thee
Floundered, here I am, nothing to offer to other
    journeymen;
And I chose a path that was chosen for me;
And have gained nothing,
For I sit here fruitless,
After the journeymen

RUBIES AND DIAMONDS

Down in the quarry, the
colliers decide
Will they steal the rubies
or the diamonds
And from what I've experienced
with despise,
I prefer the tang of rubies,
nothing else abides
But if I had lived to prosper;
if I had been wise
I'dve stuffed my pockets with
diamonds,
To evade loathing, every time

WE CALL THAT SPRING

How constantly and consistently snow settles,
O'er the blades of grass that are unburdened by this
Which freezes all life in too little time
Especially, when Jack Frost has a deep sermon to sing

As to facilitate the cold in a maximized manner
We implant comfort into suddenness
To where even the trees rest with sanction
And the Fall leaves rest

And yet, the ordeal settles as well,
For Winter arises into its own unique form
Melting away what was hidden before us
We call that Spring

EXERTION ONCE MORE

I so desire to begin my exertion once more
The notion, the collected works, the
distinctiveness of each word
The most night or day, the concerted feed for
the fire
And the image, does entail, as to the mind
prevails
to which I must pursue in a more organized
manner,
for I am pleased with what I've done,
but not for where I am,
I would think likely later

LOVE^9.

Love is a glass casing
That encloses the heart
And blindly sings a song of enticement
And reluctantly to take part

And intricacy of the china is sheltered
And aching must be the hammer
That could replace the key of the cabinet
Which has never been enamored

I've heard glass shatter in the reins
And in the hands of the divine
Of all the glass casings in the world they could've broken,
They decided to break mine

SWANS

I know I am the least coherent when beat down
My disposition is that of an archetype
And that's easy for me to throw a fist

And I recall you do the same
Yet, you have not my permission
Just because of the swans, you find it set forth

Nor do I have the permission
For I do not understand what I truly mean
when I walk away in silence

THE ARCHITECT

Standing in the midst of relics being formed
An architect ponders rhetorics, what is worth his time
What is worth sculpting with every scar on his chest
What is misled as a deed forsaken with the rest
"I'm not worthy, you're not worthy"
Cries he as his world around him is to change
Splitting images and forced contemporary shame
He takes out his hammer just to lie it down
And walks away forever, never to be found
He walks for centuries, he regrets for miles
Somewhere stricken between the courtesy
of his own thoughts and his own desires

OF INTERMEDIATE LIFE AND COMPANY

Often, it is, that I embrace the natural alone;
For, company is lovely, but they veer me in such a way that the natural seems to be absent and becomes merely hypothetical.

I don't want to be seen appreciating something others call profound and special in a patronizing way. I have my way of getting by, as do you.

This, then, is hunger; for I often claim that I am company myself. I often find myself catching a glimpse of the woods; dreaming of submerging myself within the natural, and then my mind points me in the direction that I was heading.

These rare moments of pretension and confession display something uniquely human, yet greater than ourselves, and that is our way to get by and pray; of intermediate life and company.

THE BRIDGE

I've anointed myself the skipper of this helm
Mendacious barque, which really is a wood raft
Opaline waters blending with the rot of the wood;
As the inlet moves not an inch

And the baldcypress and the weeping willows,
Stand before the mighty oak
An old pair lie across the river, denoting itself as a dam; for
    beavers

In the menial symbiosis of man and elder green,
The wild is of but a passing glance; as the dusk wind and
    sky paint the clouds with opals,
Such as the waters; and a nearby sound of chirping from
    some longing animal,
Employing their loneliness into the vast unknown,
Such as I, for no raft is of my ideal

For the first time, since I've been bustling the realm
Of Missouri,
I've found a bridge that I can cross
Between the elder green and the ornate stream
Where my skipperness doesn't seem so humble

IN A FIELD BEHIND THY HOUSE

If I had been the flowers
And thou hath been the sun
How queer upon the garden
To have grown from nothing to one
Since I am not so fluent
With the other flowers vast
I'll respond to thy glistering rays
And return to thee at last

VENUS

I built a fine marble house: Greek
A courtyard with Venus
Right next to where the mourning doves sing
Where I could listen in serenity
Venus, I'll name you Venus
One could mistake you for a white dove
Your voice not so sorrowful
Your figure, not so ragged
There is hope

                                      Venus circles the grounds
                    Appreciating the bird bath and the fresh grass
                          The other mourning doves cry at change
               They do not appreciate the bird bath or the fresh grass
                            I relate to the mourning doves more,
                                        But I believe Venus
                                          I pray for Venus
Venus, the world will cherish you, if they listen to your song

SIMPLY REMINDS ME

When referring to Ginkgos or Japanese Maples,
I will use the phrase "In God's image,"
although my beliefs are dissonant,
my thoughts always lead back to "In God's image"
and the occasion is that God simply reminds me,
of all the greatest things; an overspread term
To which are the Ginkgos or the Japanese Maples or the
    Baobabs or the Flowering Dogwoods or the Rainbow
    Eucalyptuses (more standard Eucalyptuses will also
    provide and remain comely)
I don't find myself piously standing at the foot of my bed
    thanking God for these trees;
Instead, I piously stand at the foot of the bark and thank
    every branch and every flower,
For this is God's finest hour

WATERCOURSE

There is a bird
That speaks few words
But can sing much more
Than speak those words
And is mute in truth
But those who hear
Will tell with a spear
That noise is shrill
And so sheer

Whatever flies in the morn
Is greeted and adorned
But the bird that flies at night
Is treated with scorn
And there's no room to have won
Down the rivers run
In the race all birds fly
And the songs have been unsung

XIX

I'm a reflection of you! How do you do?
I know you as much as you'd like to choose—
We're merely one, for you're a mirror too—
don't speak out loud
They'd be properly confused.

How asking to be an expression.
Too authentic, like one's eyes!
To fabricate that you're not a mirror—
does not come as a surprise.

IN LIMERENCE

In Limerence
You bore me, with mercy and
ecstasy
With no intentions besides
studying what could happen
And in the mounds of
decadence,
I have caught adrift,
For I too have a fever of the
utmost certainty
That I am infatuated with
something greater than myself
And so I can never bestow a
genuine fancied hand
For this is limerence

EVENING AFFAIRS

As I settled upon a book, at some silent place
Returning to another escape of poems,
with voices of winds that whisp around the meaning of a
    word
A thought arose before my mind almost in physical form
Reluctant in creation
Heavy is the thing,
That perplexes my everlasting notion
Dost thou think of me when in course for inspiration ?
Dost my words carry enchanting visions much as those
    prior to me
With an envious but longing finger pointing towards a
    ghosts old world
But the ghost said before me,
"Orators of my time have not one word to say back,
for war, pestilence, conquest, and death, and they art
    merely the lamb;
but thy time, thou art the lamb"

"Is that all there is", continued I
"I also run from both the lamb and the terrors of our times,
for there is nothing greater worrisome than ancient thought
    that stampedes on modern distress
For our agitations are hidden in plain sight, and coping is
    the greatest crime, which has been planted by the likes
    of yourself,
Dost thou understand?"
Out of the flash of my voice, the ghost was gone
No longer did I view the page blank,
for I had answered my own question

MOURNING DOVES MAKE FOOLS

There is a sound that excites a welcoming of Spring
A reverberated omen, the voice of a mourning dove
What makes each morning willing
They spread the good word throughout the brook
Where many of them reside,
And those; a faction of life, can hear
Those of receipt penury
Though whenever they spread the good word,
It is empathetic
Where Spring is Genesis;
And is squandered, a vicious cycle
For the mourning doves occasionally visit those that reside,
And often, those that reside mishear
On good days; those that reside are correct,
And curse the doves out,
For the word is nothing but mournful
And the mourning doves make fools

WILD WIGHT

Not for thy faith, body, or avarice, wild wight,
Not for thy titled descent, nor thy name,
Thou lose not a morsel from plight or adulation,
Not thee - tis our assemblage bound, so sought after;
Uniform be our atonement, efforts to be our select,
State to be succor, life to be well loved,
These essentials do I honor - wish thee would implement,
But as thy era calls for rigorous means:
Then nae, O taciturn! My lord's crown on the upright!

A POEM TO A SUBSEQUENT MAN

I; not even enduring a score
Have surmounted the harness of life,
Barely any loss, barely any idiosyncrasy,
Not many a heartache, not many a road traveled yet,
It's all there, before me,
Leading me to many learning years;
And I can see the roads I've been travelin on,
Full of vagaries that tease my unburdened tranquility;
Some good, some bad
Like most if not all people; this thought eschews my
    pioneering desires
And I lament
Realizing that people like me course people like me
But I won't indulge until much later;
The much later that is old age,
And I will be prepared to state:
I'd be willing to do it all over again

DIVERSION

This excruciating diversion, this winter,
like the rebuilding of the Versailles,
and stonemasons, bricklayers at blemished walls
We are too tired and uncaring to start once more
With staffs in our grasp,
And longing for our staffs, we know we don't know

Tired by the sirens and the fires burning
Like dust that never settles
And no one has a vacuum
Walking along some barren tunnel not in
And students of better education are unheard of and are
    the oppressed

We have learned beauty in sorrow
But we cannot see through the veil of liars
And winter seems to always be in season
And December is in the past

CARDINALS

Seizing the Spring in her meandered nose
The cardinal has gone to roam
Leaving merely only her unsolicited tracks
For the summer to discover

I've told all to catch a longer glimpse of the cardinal
To have her imprinted to some medium
But you countered
She is only a scarlet blue bird
Who appreciates dirt as much as you do
So far and high
From our prejudiced perception

I had flicked a thumb in your direction
But you only tied a scarf around your head and vanished
The cardinals wings are of fire and ash
And we are so ruthlessly lucky
Not to seem hopeless
When she melts ice against the earth

Now her futile den of twigs and leaves
Mirrors that of pending cancers
Amongst the watchtowers
For I don't know what is next
I don't know when she will fly back home
And you interrogate me, a longing soul
You ask whether we should entice her
And be furious and hold a grudge
Or draft a nominal crown made of thorns
But also of emeralds

But don't look so weary of her
When in this canvas sky
The flights that many of cardinals have taken
Still engraving and painting old routines
Or of when the cardinal lingers
And she feels anointed in protection and familiarity
The cardinal has flown from her nest
And we are honored
And we look forward to every Spring

A NOT SEEN ACUMEN

He is no dissident - separated, separating.
No one has given him praise for thought.
His agitation is not seen as shrewd, but rather fragmented
On the behalf of those that don't know him, he'd say;
A discernible straightness of him, yet lacking posture.
He doesn't fall behind or progress ahead,
He stands to the side and infers and reckons
To those that run and fall.
He pursues a pursuer who pursues pursuing
Another who is apathetic, more honest, same difference.
Anybody that pursues him, he says, is pursuing what he
    does not know.
His dissidence is pursuing what is eternal.
It is his own dreams that control his present,
And lest he enjoys pursuing what is not certain and cannot
    be determined by anyone besides time,
I recommend not being wrong.

BY HEAVEN

There, the earth so seemingly gay upon the barren sky
For nothing so unreachable shall stay
No habitation kneels on the bluff of necessity,
No winged animal feels so liberated by Heaven,
The horizon rim is merely at rest - benefitted and beneficial
When our days were filled with ambition and hope,
And unfortunately, we have learned to cope,
Yet we despise our progression-and rightfully so,
To each his own to know that when the ink is dry,
More creation of his alibi as to why he let the Heavens die
    - fall,
And why, by Heaven, we have settled over rubble - nigh,
And by Heaven, the prospect that we can pave anew is
    high.

THE OSTLER AND STEED

Once when the snow began to melt into the Earth, the rest of the year was beginning to bloom in the form of petals,
Of various colors and chemistry;
With dissimilar sense; not prompted before them prior to the dawn of man
And when man is departed, none shall implement the names given
And the Earth shan't lose a morsel of meaning
These words were spoken never before;
And in solitary construction; for man is the most lonely
And to think that we will be deserted when the Earth drifts from us
I am of mankind; an ostler upon the inn
Who tends to the stallions and mares; to share them upon the occupation of draft horse, carthorse, packhorse, you name it
There was this one horse, rather a bronco, who was the most vigorous and resistant; would make a great wild one:
The horse named Steed
I donned my coal jacket in a hesitant matter as I heard galloping outside my kitchen,
And fair enough, he was there,
Rustling through the half-melted snow, kicking it up into a fine mist
I grabbed my crop and scurried outside, and made it about halfway through the snow before I cried out,
'Hey! Steed! Come hither! Come here, baby!'

I saw him effortlessly dance around the broken fences and
   the trees;
Like a marionette with poor strings, like the rain upon the
   bank
No centered sight captured his wild or grace
I shouted once again and he looked at me, in the midst of
   his outing
He snorted at me. And then he fled through the gates and
   down the dirt path; lifting the snow into the sky as a
   blanket, becoming much of what the snow-patched
   path wasn't, a staple of winter,
Like a silhouette behind a waterfall paired with rocks.
My husband had run out of the house just to see the
   smallest glimpse of the Stallion,
'I think he knew it was his time. He isn't wild, he isn't tied
   to a great occupation, he's tied to the Winter. He's
   been like this every season, and I guess the latch must
   have broken. I doubt he will come back; but hopefully,
   he does, and hopefully, you can finally settle down the
   crop and retire for the Winter, maybe perpetually. God
   knows you need it.'
And so that I did, I ambled back into the warm kitchen and
   sat down at the round table,
Mugging my morning coffee and persisting in my
   newspaper,
My husband retired to his armchair, where he read Brontë
   and piped some Ogdens tobacco
I couldn't sit still for very long, and so I rushed outside into
   the cold and ran to the paddock,

I eyed the other horses, they were silent and steady, then I turned to Steed's pen, and to my surprise, the lock was not broken, it was firm in place as I had last left it
I called out my husband's name,
He came rushing to me from the snow,
Wearing his morning attire,
Like me, he set his eyes on Steed's pen,
'Well, I'll be damned. Poor ol' Steed, it was his due, and he knew it. I wonder what made him stay for as long as he did, and I wonder if he'll be satisfied in the wild.'

About the Author

Dashiell Grey is an American writer of poetry and plays thus far.

Currently attending Collingswood High School in New Jersey, he has many other passions such as writing music, reading, making art, and traveling with friends, family, and even his dog.

An always fascinated person, Grey is constantly learning as much as he is writing. He is inspired by those who were once inspired and so forth.

To learn more about works by Dashiell Grey visit our website at www.smallpotatoespress.com

Made in the USA
Monee, IL
21 December 2023